Famous Court Cases That Became Movies

WITCHCRAFT ON TRIAL

From the
**Salem
Witch Hunts**
to
The Crucible

Maurene J. Hinds

Enslow Publishers, Inc.
40 Industrial Road
Box 398
Berkeley Heights, NJ 07922
USA
http://www.enslow.com

Library of Congress Cataloging-in-Publication Data

Hinds, Maurene J.
    Witchcraft on trial : from the Salem witch hunts to the Crucible / Maurene J. Hinds.
        p. cm. — (Famous court cases that became movies)
    Includes bibliographical references and index.
    Summary: "Examines the witchcraft trials in Salem Village, including the young
        girls' accusations, the hearings and trials, and the inspiration for the movie,
        The Crucible"—Provided by publisher.
    ISBN-13: 978-0-7660-3055-8
    ISBN-10: 0-7660-3055-5
        1. Trials (Witchcraft)—Massachusetts—Salem—Juvenile literature.
    2. Witchcraft—Massachusetts—Salem—History—Juvenile literature.
    3. Salem (Mass.)—History—17th century—Juvenile literature. 4. Salem
    (Mass.)—Social conditions—Juvenile literature. 5. Miller, Arthur,
    1915–2005. Crucible. 6. Trials (Witchcraft) in literature. I. Title.
    KFM2478.8.W5H56 2009
    133.4'3097445—dc22

                                                    2008044550

Printed in the United States of America

10 9 8 7 6 5 4 3 2 1

To Our Readers:
We have done our best to make sure all Internet Addresses in this book were active and
appropriate when we went to press. However, the author and the publisher have no
control over and assume no liability for the material available on those Internet sites or
on other Web sites they may link to. Any comments or suggestions can be sent by e-mail
to comments@enslow.com or to the address on the back cover.

♻ Enslow Publishers, Inc., is committed to printing our books on recycled paper. The
paper in every book contains 10% to 30% post-consumer waste (PCW). The cover
board on the outside of each book contains 100% PCW. Our goal is to do our part to help
young people and the environment too!

Illustration Credits: The Art Archive/Culver Pictures, p. 36; Everett Collection, pp. 1, 4, 22,
77, 81, 84, 86, 90; Granger Collection, New York, pp. 16, 18, 62; Library of Congress,
p. 65; North Wind Picture Archives, pp. 44, 73; courtesy of Peabody Essex Museum,
Salem, MA, pp. 10, 27, 52, 59, 69.

Cover Illustrations: Gavel—Digital Stock; courthouse logo—Artville; movie still from
The Crucible—Everett Collection.

CONTENTS

A scene from the film *The Crucible* shows the girls of Salem Village who accused their neighbors of practicing witchcraft.

Chapter 1

Satan in Salem

After a long, harsh New England winter, the people of Salem Village faced a crisis. In a chilly, damp meeting-house, two women sat accused of witchcraft, a crime punishable by death.

Three men questioned a slave and a group of girls. All of them, they claimed, had experienced the most horrible torments, caused by the accused women. Tension filled the room. Was there enough evidence against the women to take them to court for the crime of witchcraft? The officials, and the room full of people watching, wanted to find out.

A strange affliction had affected the community for several months. Young girls, teenagers, and some adults had come down with a mysterious ailment. Sometimes the girls ran around their homes as if flying, yelling, "Whoosh! Whoosh! Whoosh!" Other times their bodies froze in place, making it impossible for them to move. Or they ran toward a fireplace, ready to jump in if not held back by grown men.

In the courtroom, Magistrate John Hathorne first asked the accusers about Goody Cloyce, one of the women under suspicion. "Who hurt you?" Hathorne asked.

John Indian, a slave belonging to the village's minister, answered first. "Goody Proctor first, and then Goody Cloyce."

"What did she do to you?"

"She brought the book to me." He meant the book of the devil. Witches asked their victims to make their mark in it (many could not write) in blood. This mark showed their loyalty to the devil.

> A strange affliction had affected the community for several months. Young girls, teenagers, and some adults had come down with a mysterious ailment.

John Hathorne spoke louder. "John! Tell the truth, who hurts you? Have you been hurt?"

John Indian described how the specter (a spirit or ghostly image) of Goody Proctor tried to choke him. She also brought the book. He described how Goody Cloyce visited him many times and pinched him so hard, he bled.

"Oh! You are a grievous liar!" Goody Cloyce responded to the accusations.

Forms of Address

Among the Puritans, "Goodwife" and "Goodman" were used with names, similar to our use of "Mrs." and "Mr." "Goody" was a shortened form of "Goodwife."

Mary Walcott, one of the afflicted girls, described how she, too, had been visited by Goody Cloyce. As she spoke, she cried out, seemingly in agony, twisting and writhing in pain. Community members watched in amazement and fear. They knew the cause of Mary's pain: witchcraft.

Mr. Hathorne turned to Abigail Williams, another of the afflicted girls. "Abigail Williams!" he yelled to be heard over Mary's torments and the crowd of observers. "Did you see a group at Mr. Parris's house eat and drink?"

"Yes, sir. That was their sacrament," Abigail answered.

"How many were there?"

"About forty, and Goody Cloyce and Goody Good were their leaders."

"What was the sacrament?"

"They said it was our blood, and that they drank it twice that day."

The crowd gasped.

Mary Walcott, able to speak again, described how she had seen a white man, a leader of the witches.

So great was his power that the witches trembled in fear. She named some of the witches she saw in the group, including Goody Cloyce.

Amid the shouts and accusations, Goody Cloyce could take no more. Unable to defend herself, she asked for some water and fainted.

Some of her accusers fell into fits, shrieking in pain. "Oh! Her spirit is gone to prison to her sister!" they cried out, watching Goody Cloyce's specter leave her body and fly out of the room.

Mr. Hathorne turned to Elizabeth Proctor. "Elizabeth Proctor! You understand you are charged with the sundry acts of witchcraft. What do you say to it? Speak the truth, and you that are afflicted, you must also speak the truth, as you will answer to God another day. Mary Walcott! Does this woman hurt you?"

"I never saw her so as to be hurt by her," Mary answered. She had not seen the specter of Goody Proctor.

"Mercy Lewis! Does she hurt you?" She could not answer, as her mouth had frozen shut.

Mr. Hathorne addressed another accuser. "Ann Putnam, does she hurt you?" Ann could not speak either.

Mr. Hathorne tried again. "Abigail Williams! Does she hurt you?" Abigail's hand was thrust in her mouth.

Mr. Hathorne then addressed John Indian. "John! Does she hurt you?"

The only accuser able to answer, John Indian, said, "This is the woman that came in her shift and choked me."

"Did she ever bring the book?"

"Yes, Sir."

"Are you sure of it?" Hathorne asked again.

"Yes, Sir."

From the crowd, John Proctor, Goody Proctor's husband, muttered, "If I had John Indian in my custody, I would soon beat the devil out of him!"

Mr. Hathorne asked Goody Proctor to answer the accusations.

"It is not so," she said. "There is another judgment," she told her accusers.

Abigail and Ann became hysterical, crying out and yelling, "Look! There is Goody Proctor upon the beam!" Pointing to the wooden beams above, the girls shrieked. They also said Goodman Proctor was on the beam. Watching the specters above, the accusers had grievous fits, tortured by those attacking them from above.

Mr. Hathorne yelled above the chaos. "Ann Putman! Who hurt you?"

"Goodman Proctor, and his wife, too!" she answered.

"He is taking Mrs. Pope's feet!" an accuser yelled.

Mr. Hathorne turned to Goodman Proctor. "What do you say Goodman Proctor, to these things?"

Goodman Proctor stood to defend himself. "I know not, I am innocent!" A strong man, he spoke with force. Mrs. Pope started shrieking and convulsing.

John Proctor was taken into custody. The afflicted girls continued convulsing, shrieking, and swinging their arms. They tried to defend themselves against the specters of Goody Cloyce and John and Elizabeth Proctor. Some of the girls offered to touch the defendants to see if the fits would stop. If they did, it would mean the specter had returned to its owner. Abigail reached out to strike Goody Proctor. As her hand drew

An illustration from an 1892 magazine shows the afflicted girls, two women they accused, and the judges who conducted the trials.

close, it unclenched from a fist and gently landed upon Elizabeth Proctor's hood.

"They burn! My fingers burn!"

Ann Putnam dropped to the floor.

The chaos continued. The defendants could not recite the Lord's Prayer correctly—a sure sign of witchcraft.

As the questioning came to a close, Sarah Cloyce, Elizabeth Proctor, and John Proctor were taken away to jail, where they would await their trial.[1]

This narrative, based on transcripts and a timeline presented in *The Salem Witch Trials*, gives an idea of the pretrial events.[2] What exactly happened, no one knows. The records do show a scene of chaos, outbursts, and accusations in the pretrials. The official trials resulted in nineteen hangings. One man was pressed to death, and several others died in jail.[3] Many accused spent months in cold, dank jails, where they had little food or clothing and were perhaps tortured.

The Crucible

Arthur Miller's play *The Crucible*, and the movie made from it, are based upon the events that occurred in Salem, Massachusetts, in 1692. Miller fictionalized many aspects of the historical events but wrote a story showing how people act when dealing with feelings of guilt. His work also shows the power of a group against individuals. The story centers on John Proctor; his wife, Elizabeth; and Abigail Williams. Many other characters in the story are also based upon real people. Miller was inspired to write the play by events taking place in the United States in the 1950s.

The Salem witch trials are a fascinating part of American history. They have fed imaginations and caused many to question how and why such an event could happen. How could a group of mostly young girls take control of a community and send so many people to their deaths?

The number of condemned witches in Salem was much lower than that in Europe, where tens of thousands of people died (the exact numbers are not known); however, the Salem trials happened toward the end of the witch craze. Because the people involved kept many records, more information is available about these trials than most witchcraft cases. This has allowed historians to review the events to try to determine how they unfolded and why. The trials show an interesting side to human behavior. They also influenced the types of evidence that could be allowed in a legal trial.

The Crime
of Witchcraft

What is witchcraft? The answer to this question differs depending on who answers. People have used various activities that some consider witchcraft or forms of magic. The lines that separate magic, folklore, sorcery, and witchcraft can be hard to define, and have changed over time. For example, what some people call witchcraft today is much different from how European cultures defined it a few hundred years ago.

How did the idea of witchcraft begin? Throughout history there have been people who have wanted to see into the future or cure a disease. Various rituals developed to help people do just that—see or change future events. Witch doctors helped cure disease, and sorcerers helped see into the future. Even today, many people check their horoscopes daily, consult psychics, or use tarot cards to see what lies ahead.

A person's ability to see into the future, to treat illnesses with herbs, or to affect the natural order of things was at times both sought after and feared. For some, a fine line rested between helping and harming. Witches, or what people later associated with witchcraft in Europe and New England, crossed that line.

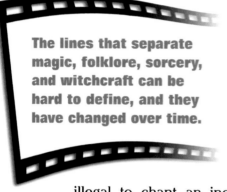

The lines that separate magic, folklore, sorcery, and witchcraft can be hard to define, and they have changed over time.

Crimes of sorcery and witchcraft date back to the earliest written records. Early Roman law, outlined in the Twelve Tables (451–450 B.C.E.), stated that it was illegal to chant an incantation with the purpose of harming another.[1] Over time Christianity became the dominant religion in Europe. Earlier beliefs (such as worshipping multiple gods) were considered dangerous by some, which also led to changes in the law. The Roman emperor Constantine (280?–337 C.E.) declared Christianity to be the state religion.[2] Not all agreed with this decision, however, and not everyone practiced religion the same way. This led to the issue of heresy.

A heretic is someone who holds differing opinions from those of the church or someone who rejects the "true" or legal faith. Among the practices considered heretical were the practice of witchcraft and sorcery.

The Roman Catholic Church determined that heretics should be prosecuted and punished, often by death. Pope Innocent III declared in 1198 that those who continued to practice heresy, even after being excommunicated or shunned by the Church, should be put to death by burning.[3] In 1231 Pope Gregory IX decided that heretics should serve a life sentence in prison if they confessed and repented. For those who did not confess, the punishment was death.[4] By 1484 Pope Innocent VIII declared heresy punishable by death.[5]

These events are often referred to as the Inquisition. It marks the early years of the "witch craze" in Europe.[6] The term witch craze refers to the time in Europe when the hunting and punishing of witches reached its highest level. The practice of burning witches began in continental Europe. In England, where the Puritans originated, the punishment was hanging.

From the early 1300s, fears of witchcraft had taken hold in Europe and surrounding areas. By 1450 the witch craze had started; it lasted for over two hundred years, peaking between 1560 and 1660.[7] The Salem witchcraft trials took place at the end of that period.

Who Was a Witch?

The description of a witch evolved over several hundred years. However, there were some basic defining characteristics. Many of these influenced the views of the Salem community. A witch was usually a woman (although in Salem many men were accused of witchcraft). Historians have differing views on why most of the accused were female. Some believe that it was the result of misogyny, or hatred of women. It was believed that

During the witch craze in Europe, thousands of people were executed. This engraving shows the hanging of a group of witches in Scotland in 1678.

women were more fragile than men and therefore more likely to be tempted by the devil. Historian Jeffrey B. Russell points out in *A History of Witchcraft* that another possible reason was that the devil was almost always shown as a male. Witches were thought to be sexually attracted to the devil. Therefore, if the devil was male, most of his subjects would be female. Russell says that "sexist religious assumptions are the most important reason" why witches were female.[8] Male figures had the most power in religion, whether for good or evil. Christ was male, and so was the devil. Women did not hold as much power; they did not have as many positive figures (such as the Virgin Mary) nor as great an ability to fend off the devil. An early book on witchcraft, the *Malleus Maleficarum* ("The Hammer of Women Who Work Harmful Magic," also translated as "The Hammer of Witches," printed in 1487[9]) implied that women were "more likely than men to be witches because they were weaker, more stupid, superstitious, and sensual," writes Russell.[10] There is no question that women were accused of, and put to death for, witchcraft much more frequently than men. Why this happened has been the subject of debate by historians.

The witch craze traveled across Europe and into England. In 1629 a group of Puritans left England for the New World to escape the religious tensions at home and begin a new, pure community. The Puritans disagreed with the Catholics on many issues, and in England there was no separation of church and state. The beliefs of the monarch determined the country's official religion.

The *Malleus Maleficarum,* an early book on witchcraft, was published in 1487. It explained how witches could be recognized and how they should be prosecuted by the authorities.

■■■■■■■■■■■■■■■■■■■■■■■■■■■■■■■■■

Witchcraft in New England

What did witchcraft mean to the people of Salem, Massachusetts? Most historians agree that the Puritans viewed witchcraft as the work of the devil. In the minds of the Puritans, people could be possessed by the devil to do evil. They could also choose to do his work by entering into an agreement, or contract, with him. The element of choice had great importance. Someone who chose to work for the devil posed more of a threat than someone possessed. The Puritans believed that every individual answered to God. To work for the devil meant to turn against God and everything that the Puritans believed. Religion did not only matter on Sunday. Puritans' beliefs were part of their daily lives. To choose the work of the devil, then, was to reject their way of life—one that held the community together.

While prayer might work for someone possessed, it might not work for someone who had a contract with the devil. In those cases, unless the person realized their wrongdoing and prayed for forgiveness, the only way to solve the problem was to eliminate the evil. The Puritans did that by hanging convicted witches.

Many Puritans believed that people who agreed to do the work of the devil joined secret groups by signing a special book. They would fly on brooms or sticks to meet with other witches and the devil. Witches were accused of cursing their neighbors, killing babies, making people and animals ill, and being intimate with the devil. Author Marilynne K. Roach describes general Puritan beliefs about witches, who were

> basically envious, resented their neighbors'
> successes, and enjoyed their misfortunes. . . . They

were shape-shifters, who changed their forms in the same way that they managed invisibility, but they also had familiar spirits—imps—in animal guise and it was often difficult to distinguish a witch from her familiar.[11]

This belief that witches had familiars, or animal spirits who did their bidding, later became important in the trials. Beliefs that witches could fly through the night also played a role, although no actual "broom riding" was reported. Many of the accusers swore that the spirits of the accused witches and/or their familiars visited them in their homes and tortured them. Many accusers also claimed to see the specters, or evil spirits, of the accused during the trials. Witches could also cause harm from a distance, using various spells and rituals. Dolls pricked with pins could cause pain in someone, for example, or a witch could cast an evil eye, with negative consequences for the person the witch looked upon.

Why Salem?

In the 1690s the people of Salem faced a number of both internal and external stressors, all of which probably had some influence on the crisis of 1692. As an English colony, the people of Salem found themselves in limbo, as their Royal Charter had expired. This left no formal law in place during the pretrials. (King William signed a new charter in October 1691; formal trials took place once the new government was put into place on May 14, 1692.) Conflicts with the French and American Indians left many people grieving family members and friends lost in gruesome battles. Some people in Salem had witnessed these events, which could easily have left psychological scars. Additionally, the tight-knit community of Salem had an influx of newcomers who had escaped war-ravaged communities. Frequent arguments over land boundaries took place. Differences between the farming and merchant communities also caused tensions to form. Many families had traditionally worked the land. This changed as the sea trades grew and developed. Lastly, the people of Salem found themselves in a position of defending traditional religious beliefs against new scientific ideas that had started to emerge.

All of these factors created uncertainty for the people of Salem. People also faced unknowns as an independent community. Salem Village, where the outbreaks occurred, was an outlying community of Salem Town. (It is now called Danvers.) In many ways Salem Village was its own community, with about five hundred residents, but was legally a part of Salem Town, several miles away. The residents paid taxes to Salem Town but did not receive any benefit from those taxes. Prior to 1689 (a few years before the witchcraft accusations) they did not have their own church, which meant they had to travel several miles to Salem Town to worship.[12] People did not have the means of travel that people use today. Even on horseback, travel could be difficult, particularly in harsh New England winters. Additionally, Salem Town was a merchant town. The people of Salem Town and the farmers of Salem Village had differing viewpoints.

On October 8, 1672, Salem Village was allowed its own church, but it was not yet a separate community.[13] The people had to pay for their own church and also pay

Witches were thought to associate with evil creatures called "familiars." Shown is a woodcut of two witches with a familiar.

taxes to larger communities such as Andover, Topsfield, and Wenham, which claimed to have control over Salem Village. Disagreements over land boundaries meant that some households were taxed by two separate communities. This caused further stress on the residents and neighborly relations.

According to many who have studied the Salem witch crisis, problems began with the building of the new church. While there are many factors that affected the outbreak of accusations, the new church played a role. Many pastors came and went. The Reverend Samuel Parris arrived in the spring of 1688.[14] Ideally, pastors would serve the same church for life. However, ongoing disputes between the residents and pastors led to several ministers coming to Salem Village only to leave within a few years. Former pastors later found themselves involved in the witch trials. One was the Reverend George Burroughs, who was later accused of witchcraft himself.

The new church enabled villagers to worship close to home. It also caused additional problems, such as the need to pay a minister. For a struggling community this could be a difficult task. Membership in the church proved to be an issue and directly affected who would pay the ministers. To become a full member, men described to the congregation a conversion experience resulting in a personal relationship with God. They stated that they had a personal covenant, or agreement, with God. (Women did this through the pastor, not in front of the congregation.) Many people who attended church were not full members. People disagreed over who was eligible to vote for a minister, who would pay, and how much. Samuel Parris was ordained as the church pastor on November 16, 1689,[15] after months of negotiations about pay and supplies such as firewood (an expensive yet much-needed supply in the cold Northeast).

During this time, legal disputes were still going on between Massachusetts and England. Increase Mather, a Boston minister, traveled to England to have the Royal Charter put back in place. He accomplished this, with several well-known men serving in official positions. Sir William Phips was named governor; William Stoughton, deputy governor; Isaac Addington, secretary; and several others were listed as councillors. This new government was sealed by King William in October 1691.[16] However, the people of Salem Village and surrounding communities would not know this for several months, until Increase Mather returned.

In the meantime, a crisis developed in Salem Village.

Chapter 3

The Path to Court: Legal Issues and Events

The Salem crisis began in January of 1692, when Samuel Parris's daughter and her cousin, who lived with the Parris family, became "ill." Nine-year-old Betty Parris and her cousin Abigail Williams (who was eleven or twelve) started acting strangely. Sometimes they apparently reacted to bites and pinches, the sources of which were unknown. Other times their bodies twisted into unnatural positions. Sometimes moving caused extreme pain, or they would be unable to speak. The symptoms grew worse, and no one knew what caused them. They were, however, similar to those described by Cotton Mather in a popular book he had written about a witchcraft case in Boston in 1688.

Parris asked Dr. William Griggs to determine the cause. He said the girls were under an "evil hand," based on their bizarre symptoms.[1] (It is possible that having no other explanation and being unable to cure the girls, the doctor decided witchcraft was the only explanation.[2]) John Hale, who had witnessed the girls, said that they twisted and turned in ways that would have been impossible to do without some outside force.[3] This made sense to Parris, as many people of the time believed in witchcraft. There was no other obvious cause of the girls' suffering—and soon after, it was not limited to those two girls.

Parris's neighbor Mary Sibley told Parris's slaves, Tituba and her husband, John Indian, to bake a cake mixed with the girls' urine. The witch cake was fed to a dog, who, according to countermagic folklore, would lead them to the cause—the witch who was causing pain.[4] The cake did not seem to work. Parris, upon hearing that this had happened, gave Mary Sibley a stern reprimand.

The Trouble Spreads

Others in the community then became ill. Ann Putman, who was twelve at the time, and her mother, Ann senior, began having similar symptoms. Seventeen-year-old Mercy Lewis, the Putnams' servant, also became afflicted, as did Mary Walcott, the Putnams' neighbor and relative. Another neighbor, seventeen-year-old Elizabeth Hubbard, fell ill, and so did Mary Warren, a twenty-one-year-old servant.

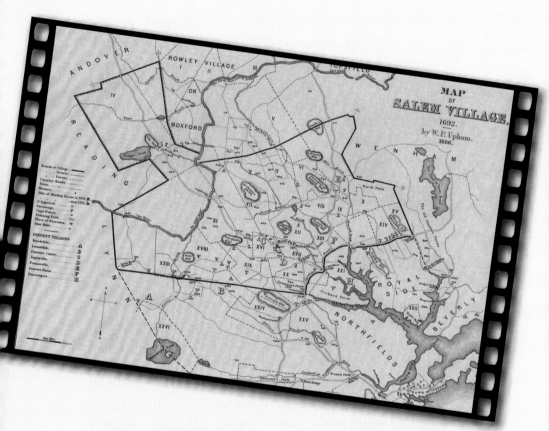

A map of Salem Village as it appeared in 1692. Legally, the community was part of Salem Town, but the two places were very different.

Did these girls have anything in common? It turns out they did, although it is important to remember that many events surrounding the Salem crisis are theories. However, the first afflictions traveled among friends and family, representing a division among Salem residents. There were two prominent families in Salem: the Porters and the Putnams. The relatives of each had arrived in Salem around the same time. Each had acquired a great deal of wealth. However, over time the Putnams started struggling in the farming business, while the Porters had success in other businesses. When Salem first looked into having its own church, the Putnams supported the idea, while the Porters did not. The Putnams later supported Reverend Parris.

For those living in Salem, the sudden outbreak must have been alarming. The girls all appeared to be in a great deal of pain and torment, and the only explanation was that evil lurked in Salem. Who caused such misery? As with many unknown issues, the people of Salem looked for answers, and they soon got them.

Experts disagree on exactly how the outbreak started. Regardless of the cause, the girls all exhibited similar strange behaviors. There were stories that the girls had taken part in some type of folk magic, but this was never proved. If they had, it would have likely been common forms of magic, such as breaking an egg white into a glass of water and seeing what shape formed. This shape might show events to come or give clues about a girl's future husband. The types of activities would be similar to using tarot cards or palm reading to look into one's future today. They probably did not take part in rituals out in the woods as shown in the movie *The Crucible*. However, if they did use some type of folk magic, the guilt may have been too much to bear. The Puritans strictly prohibited this type of activity. Did the girls feel guilty over their actions, and as a result behave strangely? Or were they under the influence of something bigger and much more terrifying? Was someone controlling them? It turns out someone very close to the girls may have had an influence.

Tituba and her husband, John Indian, came with Samuel Parris when he took over the church in Salem Village. Parris had failed at business in Barbados before coming to Salem. He did, however, come to own Tituba and John Indian somewhere along the way. Although many records refer to Tituba as an Indian, she proba-bly did not come from New England. Mary Beth Norton, author of *In the Devil's Snare: The Salem Witchcraft Crisis of 1692*, argues that she was probably a Spanish Indian from Florida or Georgia's Sea Islands.[5] Regardless of Tituba's origins, however, Norton argues that she looked like the American Indians familiar to New Englanders—the same people who threatened to attack at any moment. She helped take care of Betty Parris and Abigail Williams. It is possible that she taught the girls some of her own "magical" customs. As such, she served as the perfect scapegoat. However, the girls also named two other women.

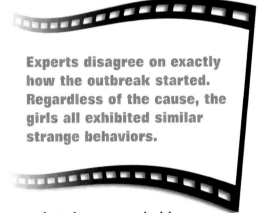

Experts disagree on exactly how the outbreak started. Regardless of the cause, the girls all exhibited similar strange behaviors.

Betty and Ann Putnam, Jr., accused Tituba, Sarah Osborne, and Sarah Good of torturing them with witchcraft. Osborne and Good were local residents—considered outcasts by some in the community. Sarah Osborne was the subject of controversy when she married one of her servants after her first husband died. The servant was much younger than she. They also had some legal issues with the Putnams that were still ongoing when the witchcraft crisis began.[6] Sarah Osborne had stopped attending church due to poor health.

Sarah Good had a husband who did not help her and had very little money. She also had two children to care for: a baby and a four-year-old daughter, Dorcas. Some regarded her as a town beggar. She acted rude to those who did not help her. Her neighbor had already suspected her of witchcraft.

All three women fell outside the norms of Puritan society. Tituba was a slave with an unknown background. Sarah Osborne and Sarah Good were not regular churchgoers, and they had some disputes with the afflicted girls' families. As Norton mentions in her book (as do other experts), those accused often fit a similar pattern. They were outsiders or had differences with the families of the accusers. These patterns continued throughout most of the crisis.

Legal Proceedings Begin

Official complaints of witchcraft were brought against these first three women on February 29, 1692.[7] To determine if enough evidence existed to go to trial, the women were brought before a public hearing, where they faced their accusers. Thomas Putnam, his brother Edward, Joseph Hutchinson, and Thomas Preston formally accused Sarah Good, Tituba, and Sarah Osborne (the afflicted girls, being female and underage, could not legally accuse their tormentors). Why the pretrials were held publicly is not known, although Norton argues that it may have been public interest.[8] In the small community nearly everyone (if not everyone) would have heard about the girls' odd behaviors and afflictions.

John Hathorne and John Corwin were two of the community's magistrates, officials allowed to carry out the laws. These two men heard the first complaints against the women made by Thomas and Edward Putnam, Joseph Hutchinson, and Thomas Preston. Hathorne took the lead in the pretrial hearings. He also played a primary role in the later trials. Because the legal issues of the times were uncertain, Hathorne used traditional Bay Colony law. Norton writes, "The 1648 *Laws and Liberties of Massachusetts* had defined a witch as one who 'hath or consulteth with a familiar spirit.' (Such familiars, frequently in the shapes of animals, were believed to link witches to the devil and to suck nourishment from their bodies.)"[9]

The goal of the pretrials was to make the accused confess to witchcraft. This process developed during the European witch crisis. In Europe, torture had been used to make accused witches confess. Whether or not torture occurred in Salem is unclear, although evidence suggests that some people were tortured in prison while awaiting their trials.

When the crisis began in Salem, the idea of "innocent until proven guilty" did not exist. This concept would enter the American legal system much later. Instead, the people of Salem seemed convinced that witchcraft could be the only explanation. A confession would confirm this. They only needed to find and question the correct people. It appears that in Hathorne's mind (and in the minds of many in the community), they had identified the witches.

Hathorne proceeded with zeal to get the women to confess to witchcraft. His task was not always an easy one. To get confessions and other information, he often used leading questions. He assumed guilt and phrased questions to make the accused agree or disagree. The questions would lead the accused in a certain direction. For example, he would ask questions such as, "Why did you do that?" or "Who made you act that way?"

Puritans believed they had a personal covenant, or agreement, with God. Puritans needed to live and behave in ways that supported their agreement with God. They had to live honest lives and fulfill their promise to God through their daily actions. If they broke a promise to God, they would be destined for hell. One way to break a promise to God was to lie. This idea would play an important role in the trials. However, human nature also played a role. The accused may have been proud and concerned about their personal integrity—this is only natural. There are also times when people act differently than they normally would in order to survive. All of these reactions happened during the Salem witch crisis.

The Pretrials

On March 1, 1692, when the questioning began, the first two women brought before the officials denied any wrongdoing. The first testimonies were in public, and the rest were presumably conducted by the magistrates in the jail.

Sarah Good was the first woman questioned. Hathorne asked her what evil spirit she was familiar with. She said none. He also asked, as noted in the transcripts from the trials, "Why [do] you hurt these children?"[10] She again denied hurting them. When the

Disorder in the Court

Outbursts by the accusers and audience during the trials are used in the play and the movie *The Crucible*. The girls scream out, showing apparent signs of pain and injury. It is likely that those in attendance also responded to what they saw. Beginning with this pretrial and throughout the crisis, the courts and examinations were spectacles of loud outbursts, screams, and leading questions. Would these types of outbursts be acceptable in a courtroom today? Probably not. Even while many movies are not always accurate, the idea of "order in the court" is one that does have some truth to it. In the days of the Salem witch trials, however, outbursts and other displays were common in the proceedings.

questions did not lead to a confession, Hathorne asked the afflicted children to look at Sarah Good and identify her as the person that had hurt them. The children "all did [look] upon her and said this was one of the persons that did torment them—presently they were all tormented."[11]

As Norton writes, this method of determining guilt would be another important part of the trials. When the girls looked at Sarah Good and identified her, they all acted hysterically, as if she were hurting them at that exact moment. At that time, Sarah Good stated that she was not the one hurting the girls, but that it was Sarah Osborne who tormented them.

Next Hathorne questioned Sarah Osborne. Hathorne used the same type of questions, asking, "What evil spirit have you familiarity with?" Osborne replied, "None." He also asked, "Why [do] you hurt these children?" and she said, "I [do] not hurt them."[12] When Hathorne asked the girls if Sarah Osborne had tormented them, "every one of them said that this was one of the [women] that did afflict them. . . ."[13]

No Presumption of Innocence

The officials assumed guilt and aggressively questioned those on trial. The accused faced an audience of their neighbors, many of whom also believed they were guilty. The afflicted girls screamed out, accused the women and men on trial of hurting them, and seemed to writhe in pain. All of this could be unsettling to someone on trial for witchcraft, which came with a severe penalty. Norton writes of the trials:

> Four distinct elements combined to create an unstable, often explosive mixture: the magistrates, assuming guilt; the accused, struggling to respond to the charges; the afflicted, demonstrating their torments; and the audience, actively involving themselves in the exchanges by offering information and commentaries.[14]

In other words, this was not a scene of a contemporary courtroom, where innocence is presumed, witnesses are questioned in a mostly quiet room, and judges oversee the proceedings to ensure that they are conducted in an orderly manner. Norton also mentions another common issue throughout the trials: Spouses and close relatives often made remarks about another's guilt or accused them outright. Both Sarah Good's and Sarah Osborne's husbands expressed doubts about their innocence. The women were no match for their accusers. Defending themselves without a lawyer, they were outnumbered.

Tituba's Testimony

After the questioning of the first two women, Hathorne questioned Tituba. Her testimony, although very early in the crisis, proved to be important. At first she denied any wrongdoing. Hathorne asked what evil spirit she had familiarity with and why she hurt the children. She responded, "I do not hurt them."[15] However, she then said that the devil hurt them and quickly added that the devil had come to her and made her serve him. This in itself stunned the audience, as she said what the other two women had not—that the devil was at work in Salem. However, Tituba did not stop with that. She told Hathorne that "[four] women sometimes hurt

Tituba, a slave belonging to Samuel Parris, was at the center of the witch frenzy. She confessed to practicing witchcraft and implicated many others. This illustration of Tituba in the forest was done in 1880.

the children."[16] She named Sarah Good and Sarah Osborne. She said they told her if she did not hurt the children, they would hurt Tituba. She then confessed to hurting the children, saying that she would not do it anymore. She said that a man had come to visit her, telling her to serve him. He promised her pretty things if she agreed.

Tituba described the many familiars of the man and the other women accused. She described how she flew on a stick with them to harm the afflicted girls. She followed this with elaborate tales of how she and the other women hurt the girls. If she had not agreed to help, the others would have cut off her head. She confessed, but said she harmed the girls out of fear for her own life. The devil controlled her. By stating these words, she said what Hathorne and many in the audience wanted to hear. She also left room for her own innocence. After all, she did not want to do these things but had no choice. The devil had threatened her, she said, forcing her to do his work and that of the other women.

Many historians agree that her statement was, although dramatic, very clever. She placed the guilt on others beside herself and, in the end, escaped death. Those who confessed were not sent to the gallows. Some historians argue that the reason a confession did not lead to hanging was because once a person confessed, he or she could ask God for forgiveness. Also, the torments suffered by the girls stopped as soon as Tituba, and later others, confessed. As stated in the transcripts, the afflicted girls "were grievously distressed until the said Indian began to confess & then they were immediately all quiet the rest of the said Indian [woman's] examination."[17]

Another key part of Tituba's "confession" was that she named others as well, just not directly. By the end of her tale, the last of which was probably told from jail, Tituba said that she had signed her mark in the devil's book. She said she had seen the names of the other two women as well, which the devil had shown her. This again implied that Sarah Good and Sarah Osborne were guilty. Tituba said she had seen nine marks in the devil's book but did not know who made the other marks. This left plenty of room for new accusations.

Why did the people of Salem Village believe Tituba's incredible story? One reason may be that Tituba began showing signs of the affliction herself. Once she had named the other witches, the reasoning went, they tormented Tituba for revealing their secrets. The Reverend John Hale, who later wrote about the crisis, thought that Tituba's stories were believable because she had been consistent. He thought that if she had been lying, her stories would have been changed when questioned again later in jail.[18] Whatever the reasons, many people in Salem Village seemed to believe that something was amiss, whether witchcraft or something else. And while no one knows how much of Tituba's stories made it to the ears of the accusers, the records show that three more persons were soon named as witches. While some people expressed doubt about the accusations later in the trials, no one seemed to speak out in defense of the accused in these early stages of the crisis.

By this time, the magistrates had learned that Sir William Phips was the new governor. Official trials for

The Character of Abigail Williams

In the movie *The Crucible*, Winona Ryder played Abigail Williams, who was eleven or twelve in 1692. Ryder was in her mid-twenties when the movie was filmed, and the character she played was seventeen. In the movie version, Abigail Williams has had an affair with John Proctor, one of the men accused of witchcraft in real life. Arthur Miller, who wrote both the play and the movie script based on his play, obviously took some liberties with these characters (and several other historical facts). The real John Proctor was sixty; in the play and movie Miller changed his age to thirty-five. Additionally, in the movie Abigail leaves on a boat, but in the historical records not much is written about her after the initial fits of hysteria.

such serious offenses could not begin until his return. Magistrates Hathorne and Corwin continued the pretrial questioning to determine if any cases should go to court when possible. As Norton argues, the magistrates had to do something. A crisis was certainly beginning to unfold.[19] They needed to act with caution, however. The men proceeded with the witch hunt.

Chapter 4

On What Grounds? Evidence and Testimony in Court

More accusations soon followed the first three. Dorcas Good, Sarah Good's young daughter, started biting and scratching at Ann Putnam, Jr. Another woman was also said to be tormenting Ann Putnam, Jr. She was Elizabeth Proctor, the wife of John Proctor. Her grandmother had been accused of witchcraft about thirty years earlier (she had been acquitted). The names of these two individuals may not have surprised the people in Salem Village. After all, each had some relation to an accused witch, and people knew that witchcraft followed family lines. However, the next person named by Ann Putnam,

Jr., was a member of the church: Martha Corey. Martha had been a widow prior to marrying her current husband, Giles, who had been widowed twice. This was not unusual for the time, as life was harsh and survival difficult. Prior to the accusations, Martha Corey had been an upstanding member of the church.

When questioned about the apparition that afflicted her, Ann Putnam, Jr., appeared to be suddenly struck blind. Was this yet another affliction, or was Putnam faking? No one knows for sure, but it put Martha Corey in danger. When the magistrates later arrived at Corey's house to question her, she said that she knew the reason for their visit. In the small village word could have easily traveled to her that she had been named by Ann Putnam, Jr. When speaking with the magistrates, Martha asked if Ann had known what Martha was wearing that day. Again, Corey may have heard that this was a method used for determining the accuracy of the accusers' stories. However, it backfired. The magistrates thought she seemed too eager with her questions about Ann. To them, her actions showed that she must have known that Ann had been unable to see. Corey then spoke of her position in the church. She said she had no sympathy for the accusers.[1]

If there was some doubt about the girls' fits, it may have come from the family of Ann Putnam, Jr., itself. Thomas Putman, Ann's father, invited Martha Corey to his house. When she entered the home, Ann junior fell into wild fits. Soon after, Mercy Lewis, the Putnams' servant, did as well. She said Martha Corey was the cause of her suffering. Mercy's afflictions were so great that she tried to fling herself into the fire. Reportedly, it took three men to hold her back.[2] Perhaps the severity of the fits convinced the adults. Ann junior bit her own tongue so hard that she could not speak for a while. Only grown men could stop Mercy's violent behavior. These extreme reactions could have ensured that the family believed the girls. Whatever the cause, Ann Putnam, Jr., Mercy Lewis, Abigail Williams, Elizabeth Hubbard, and the others continued to be affected, according to onlookers. Some older women were as well, including Ann Putnam, Sr., and Mrs. Bathshua Pope.

Martha Corey and Rebecca Nurse

Martha Corey was accused on March 12, 1692. As had happened with others, her husband expressed some doubts about her innocence. (He later changed his mind about his wife's guilt and the trials and found himself accused.) A few days later, on March 19, Rebecca Nurse found herself named.[3] On that day a former Salem Village preacher returned to town. Deodat Lawson had served the church from 1684 to 1688, and found himself drawn back to the community. The girls had said that his wife and daughter, who had died while he lived in Salem Village, had been victims of witchcraft.[4] During his stay he filled in for Samuel Parris as preacher at times. He also believed that prayer was the best cure for witchcraft. He cautioned the congregation that the devil could impersonate innocent persons, even the most outwardly devout members of the church. Martha Corey and Rebecca Nurse were both churchgoers. Parris, on the other hand, frequently preached that the devil was among the people of Salem Village. He continued to preach in this manner throughout the trials.

Martha Corey was questioned on March 21. She repeatedly denied harming the girls and stressed that she was a gospel woman. John Hathorne asked why she had mentioned her clothes when they first came to question her. He argued that she had no way of knowing that they would ask her about that (unless she was a witch). Corey explained that she had learned from her husband that this was a method that could help determine the accuracy of the accuser's claims. However, Giles Corey denied saying this, which left Martha in an unexplainable position. She then said that she had heard the girls talking about it.[5] Changing her story meant she was lying. If she lied about that, she could have lied about not being a witch. As in the other instances, the accusers, now ten of them,[6] appeared to be tormented during the questioning. Hathorne continued pressing Martha Corey to confess. She did not.

Corey repeatedly denied her guilt. The room was likely very loud, with the girls' fits, Hathorne's questions, and noise from the audience. Corey claimed that the girls were "distracted." It may have made the situation worse. Her every move seemed to affect the girls. When she bit her lip, the girls cried out. Author Marilynne Roach writes, "If she clenched her hands, her alleged victims felt it—and showed the bruises. If she slumped forward against the seat that served as a bar, they felt pain from that, too."[7] No matter what she said or did, her words and actions worked against her. Martha Corey was sent to prison.

Rebecca Nurse was seventy years old and in poor health. Partial deafness made it hard for her to hear the questions asked of her. She faced her accusers and

Martha Corey, unlike some of the women first accused, was a respected churchgoer. She repeatedly denied being a witch but was found guilty.

John Hathorne on March 21. She, too, denied any wrongdoing. As before, the girls' torments appeared to grow worse any time Nurse moved. Several historians have written that Hathorne seemed not to press Nurse as harshly as he had the others. Perhaps her standing in the community and churchgoing swayed him. At one point he said, "I pray God clear you if you be innocent, [and] if you are guilty discover you . . . ," and later, "What a sad thing it is that a church member here [and] now another of Salem, should be thus accused and charged."[8] Nurse expressed doubt about the sincerity of the girls' fits. Hathorne asked, "Do you think these suffer against their wills or not?" She replied, "I do not think these suffer against their wills."[9] Nurse seemed to be saying that the afflicted girls were faking their symptoms. She was not the only person to think this; other members of the community had expressed doubts as well.

John Proctor Speaks Up

Historian Chadwick Hansen wrote that John Proctor "expressed his opinion of the afflicted persons' testimony in no uncertain terms" to Mary Warren, his servant and one of the afflicted girls. According to Hansen, Proctor said, "If they were let alone . . . we should all be devils and witches quickly."[10] What he meant was that if left unchecked, the girls would accuse everyone. That the girls were faking their symptoms was a theory for many years after the events. (Later theories included illnesses that could cause similar reactions in the girls, or other practical explanations for some of the symptoms. Hansen says that an insect bite could have been the cause of a suddenly appearing red spot, for example.[11]) Hansen argues that Proctor's statements have been partly misunderstood, however. Proctor supposedly threatened Mary Warren with a thrashing when she first started having fits—this stopped them, at least until the next day. Hansen argues that at the time, beating was a common treatment for insanity.[12]

John Proctor's stern words toward his servant had an effect. After Proctor threatened to beat her—or actually did beat her—Mary's fits seemed to diminish. This could have negative consequences for the other afflicted girls and women, who still appeared to be experiencing torments from the spirits of those accused.[13] If they were found to be lying, they, too, could be hanged. On April 11 Elizabeth Proctor and Sarah Cloyce were questioned. During the examination John Proctor was also accused and sent to prison.[14]

Following Rebecca Nurse's examination, Reverend Parris gave a sermon expressing his view that a church member had betrayed the congregation. Upon hearing this, Sarah Cloyce, Nurse's sister, got up and left, supposedly slamming the door behind her, stunning the congregation. Hansen writes, "They were amazed, of course, not at her resentment of Parris but at her public expression of it in the midst of a church service, a virtually unheard of action in Puritan Massachusetts."[15]

Feeling Powerless?

Sarah Cloyce's actions may have shown more than just her frustration or anger. They might also shed light on the feelings of many women at the time. This, in turn, might also explain why the accusers acted out the way they did. Frances Hill writes in *A Delusion of Satan*:

> The New Englanders expected as much of the young as of adults. After earliest childhood, there was little play or amusement. There were few dolls and toys. . . . At seven or younger, children were expected to share fully in the chores of the household.[16]

Women were expected to keep house and follow the leads of their husbands, who were clearly the heads of Puritan households. Hill also writes,

> In Salem Village young women were as rigidly controlled, as powerless, and as dissatisfied as perhaps they have ever been anywhere. . . . Men and women were expected to [follow the rules of] the church, the community, and God. Young women had also to subjugate themselves to their elders and to men.[17]

Did the girls act out as a way to get power over their situation or to get the attention of their elders? Did the older women do the same? Sarah Cloyce's actions may have been expressed differently, but she, too, perhaps showed her feelings of powerlessness or disgust when she left the church. Unfortunately, she paid a high price for her actions. She, too, was accused. In the meantime, Mercy Lewis and others continued to say that they were being tormented by the spectral forms of Martha Corey and Elizabeth Proctor. John Indian, Tituba's husband, also began showing signs of the affliction. The situation was growing out of control, and the magistrates sought legal help from Boston.[18]

Ongoing Uncertainty

Increase Mather was on his way to Massachusetts from England with the new governor and Royal Charter.

This meant that all legal proceedings were still uncertain. Deputy Governor Thomas Danforth and Samuel Sewall took part in the pretrial hearings of Elizabeth Proctor and Sarah Cloyce, along with magistrates Hathorne and Corwin.

The afflicted persons were questioned first, beginning with John Indian. After the accusers described a large meeting of witches, Sarah Cloyce asked for some water and fainted. Some of the afflicted went into fits, crying out that Cloyce's spirit had left to go see her sister, Rebecca Nurse, in prison.

Elizabeth Proctor went next. Again the afflicted were asked who hurt them, but they did not speak. Only John Indian stated that Elizabeth Proctor had tried to choke him. Soon after, some of the girls found their voices and testified, again having fits. Abigail and Ann junior then accused John Proctor of hurting some of the girls. The accused were sent to prison in Boston. Throughout the interrogations, the afflicted girls reported signs of injury, claiming that the accused harmed them during the pretrials. They complained of bites, pinches, pinpricks, and other afflictions.

The next to be examined were Abigail Hobbs, Bridget Bishop, Giles Corey (Martha Corey's husband), and Mary Warren (the Proctors' maid, who had previously accused others but later recovered).

During the questioning, Abigail Hobbs, an outspoken teenager, confessed immediately to being a witch, and the accusers did not have any fits. Hobbs stated that she had met the devil a few years earlier and that he appeared to her in the shape of a "black man." Author Mary Beth Norton writes that he could have resembled a Native American, further fueling the Puritans' fears of more attacks.[19] However, when Giles Corey and Mary Warren were questioned, the accusers showed their usual reactions. Bridget Bishop had also been accused of witchcraft in 1679. The girls acted hysterical as soon as Bishop entered the room. With every move she made, they cried out in apparent agony.

Beyond Salem Village

As the events unfolded, people outside Salem Village were accused (or became accusers themselves). On April 22 several others were questioned, including Mary Easty, a well-respected woman in nearby Topsfield and sister to Rebecca Nurse and Sarah Cloyce. (Easty's case would later be a turning point in the trials.) Also questioned were Nehemiah Abbott, William and Deliverance Hobbs, Edward and Sarah Bishop, Mary Black, Sarah Wildes, and Mary English. Four more were questioned on May 2: Sarah Morey, Lydia Dustin, Susannah Martin, and Dorcas Hoar.

On May 4 a former pastor of Salem Village, George Burroughs, was arrested in Maine. He and several others were questioned on May 9. The next day George Jacobs, Sr., and his granddaughter Margaret were questioned. Margaret confessed and testified against her grandfather. That same day, May 10, Sarah Osborne died in jail. She was the first of the accused to die. The rest awaited their fates, which would soon be determined.

The Court of Oyer and Terminer

Increase Mather and the new governor, Sir William Phips, returned to Massachusetts on May 14. They had the new

Royal Charter, which brought some stability and legal grounds to the colony. It also allowed official trials to begin. Governor Phips created the Court of Oyer and Terminer, translated as "to hear and determine,"[20] on May 27. The court was designed to question and investigate the accusations of witchcraft. Phips appointed judges to oversee the trials: Lieutenant Governor William Stoughton, Nathaniel Saltonstall, Bartholomew Gedney, Peter Sergeant, Samuel Sewall, Wait Still Winthrop, John Richards, John Hathorne, and Jonathan Corwin.[21] Historian Peter Charles Hoffer writes in *The Salem Witchcraft Trials: A Legal History* that "Richards, Stoughton, and Winthrop were close personal friends of Cotton Mather and members of his church."[22]

Cotton Mather supported the trials throughout and spoke about it publicly. However, he argued that caution was necessary, and he struggled with some forms of evidence, including spectral evidence (testimony about something that a person's specter had done). The types of evidence used in the pretrials continued in the official trials. It included the testimonies of the afflicted, such as their outcries, claims of seeing spectral beings, claims of inflicted wounds, and claims of being visited by the spirits of the accused. Additional evidence included the confessions of the accused, which were not necessarily reliable. Confessions stopped the outbursts of the accused and did not lead to executions. Witches' marks were also admitted as evidence. These small marks looked like insect bites but did not hurt or bleed when touched. A "touch test" was also allowed. This test "proved" that the afflicted person was being harmed by the specter of an accused person. During a fit the accused touched the afflicted. If the fit stopped, this showed that the specter had returned to its rightful owner. Hoffer writes, "There were no hard-and-fast rules of evidence in English law. Formal rules of evidence in criminal trials had not yet evolved in 1692 and would not for many years to come."[23] He further goes on to discuss how the ideas of a modern court and jury were still in development at the time.

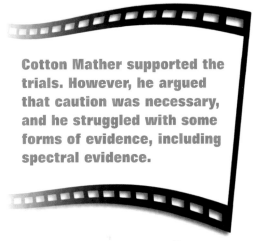

Cotton Mather supported the trials. However, he argued that caution was necessary, and he struggled with some forms of evidence, including spectral evidence.

In Salem, juries had quite a bit of freedom in how they arrived at their conclusions. Hoffer writes, "For help in instructing jurors about the invisible world, the judges looked to the ministers."[24] To them the invisible world was very real. Evidence of it was allowed in court. One other test used was the ability of the accused to recite the Lord's Prayer. According to this theory, someone who served the devil would be unable to recite the prayer.

Prior to the first hearing in the new court, several others were questioned by Hathorne, Corwin, and a new official, Bartholomew Gedney. They were Martha Carrier, John Alden, Jr., Wilmott Redd, Elizabeth Howe, and Philip English. It is possible that the reputations of these people led, in part, to the accusations against them. Bridget Bishop became the first person tried and convicted in the Court of Oyer and Terminer, on

This oil painting by T. H. Matteson shows an accused woman being examined for "witches' marks." People believed that the body of a witch would contain small marks that did not hurt or bleed when touched.

June 2, 1692. In many ways she fit a typical description of a witch. She was disliked by many, outspoken, and not a virtuous woman by Puritan standards.[25] In the small community her reputation may have been the reason why she went to trial first, although many others had been accused before her.

Bishop's trial set the stage for the remaining trials. Hoffer explains that defendants (those who had to prove themselves innocent) were at a disadvantage in the system. They could speak up for themselves, provide witnesses, and provide evidence. They could not, however, testify under oath, which the prosecutors (the accusers) could do.[26] Hoffer also notes that a trial often took less than an hour, even in capital cases where the defendant might die for his or her actions.

Additionally, legal counsel was not common, and when present, it was usually for the prosecution. In fact, it was not until the 1960s that defendants won the right to have legal counsel in criminal cases regardless of their financial or social status. This does not mean that people during the time of the Salem Witch Trials never had any legal representation. But in those days, lawyers could not charge for their services, and no one volunteered to help the accused in Salem.

Hoffer also examines the role of juries during the legal proceedings. Juries were supposed to weigh the evidence, just as they do now. Before going to trial, grand juries determined if there was enough evidence to charge someone with witchcraft. They did this using a variety of evidence, not just spectral. A trial jury then heard the case and made a decision. Generally speaking, juries in seventeenth-century New England did their jobs well. Not everyone accused of a capital offense was found guilty.

However, Hoffer notes that in the case of the Salem trials, the judges, and in particular William Stoughton, had a big influence on the court. While the grand jury made decisions separate from the judges, trial juries faced the judges in the courtroom. Fear and tensions were running high at the time. Belief in witchcraft was widespread, and many people were afraid of who would be accused next. These fears affected the judges, jurors, and spectators. The fact that the judges allowed spectral evidence, even when it was an issue of debate, also affected the mood in the courtroom. Finally, the judges seemed to have obvious opinions. Their words and reactions to the trials could have sent a clear message to the jurors: The accused were guilty (aside from those who confessed). Hoffer writes that in the Salem trials everyone brought to court was found guilty. Everyone who confessed escaped hanging unless they later took back their confession (called recanting).[27] Hoffer writes, "As important as the two kinds of juries were in these cases, the judges had more to say about the outcome of the trials than anyone else."[28]

After Bridget Bishop's trial, some people were concerned about the evidence used, the process, and the outcome. Bishop was found guilty on June 2 and hanged on June 10. The trial is in stark contrast to capital cases today, when the trial can take months. Today, if a defendant is found guilty and receives the death penalty, the case goes through an appeals process, in which the case is reviewed. It is typically many years before the sentence is carried out—not eight days.

■ ■

Spectral evidence was a key issue in the trials. Bridget Bishop, for example, found herself condemned based only on this; that is, the afflicted girls claimed to be attacked by Bishop's specter, or disembodied spirit. This, combined with her reputation, was enough for the court to convict her. This did not sit well with everyone, however, including one of the judges, Nathaniel Saltonstall. Disgusted with this type of proof, he stepped down from his position in the court. This was followed by an inquiry into the issue of the trials by several prominent ministers. Cotton Mather and several others wrote a formal reaction to the trials and situation. They delivered their opinion on June 15. While they disagreed with the use of spectral evidence, they left the issue open-ended. Cotton Mather included a paragraph at the end that supported the goals of the court and said that the court should finish what it started. This last paragraph left room for the courts to allow spectral evidence in the remaining cases. It also allowed the judges and court to save face. The ministers did not make the judges or court look bad. Instead, Cotton Mather and the others stated their hesitation but did not provide a solid opinion one way or the other. Thus, the trials continued, with spectral evidence allowed.

The first hanging did not make the fits stop. The hysteria persisted, more people throughout the surrounding areas reported afflictions, and the accusations continued. By the time the crisis started winding down several months later, over one hundred people had been accused of witchcraft throughout Salem Village and surrounding areas. Salem Village had only about five hundred occupants. After the first trial and hanging, more people stepped up to oppose the trials, but their views were overridden. Some people signed petitions in support of the accused. Rebecca Nurse had several supporters. She also raised some questions about the process that would continue to go unanswered.

Casting Doubt

Rebecca Nurse was one of several women tried toward the end of June 1692. The others were Susannah Martin, Sarah Wildes, Sarah Good, and Elizabeth Howe. Nurse's trial raised doubts about the process, more so than some of the others. Later actions of her sisters, Sarah Cloyce and Mary Easty, would continue to build doubts in the community. In some ways the trial of Rebecca Nurse, while one of the early trials, marked a beginning of the end—but the end was still many months away.

Rebecca Nurse's supporters in the community included members of the prominent Porter and Putnam families. Even though Ann Putnam, Jr., and Ann senior were major players in the accusations, some members of the Putnam family signed a petition in support of Nurse. She also had the support of her husband, other members of her family, and friends. She had a good reputation in the community and was well respected.

During the trial, Nurse answered questions honestly and logically. When questioned about being a witch, she denied that she was one but raised a good point. If the devil was at work in the community, she said, he could easily impersonate anyone of his choosing, including church members. This logic could not be denied, although the court did not admit it. Some judges believed the devil required a person's permission to impersonate him or her. Nurse said she did not know how or why the girls were afflicted. However, she denied being a witch. She also questioned why a witch, who prefers to work anonymously, would conduct witchcraft in such a public manner—in the court, where everyone could see.

Seventy years old at the time, Goodwife Nurse was not in the best of health and had hearing problems. During the examination the outbursts from the accusers continued. When the accusations of Ann Putnam, Jr., were not as influential as they had been before, her mother came to her aid and accused Nurse. Coming from an adult, the accusations against Nurse then held more weight. However, Nurse's earnest manner and convincing words must have reached the jury. They returned a verdict of not guilty. The accusers flew into hysterical fits, and the audience likely responded as well. William Stoughton reviewed the record and found a comment made by Nurse. She had said during her trial, "What, do these persons give in evidence against me now, they used to come among us."[29] Stoughton argued that her saying "they used to come among us" meant she had been in the company of witches. The jury overturned its original verdict and pronounced her guilty. When Nurse later tried to explain herself, she said that she had not been able to hear the question properly, and would have answered differently. This explanation came too late. She was sent to Gallows Hill, as it became known, on July 19. With her went Susannah Martin, Elizabeth Howe, Sarah Good, and Sarah Wildes. Hoffer writes of Rebecca Nurse, "Her demeanor was so decent and pure that many began to doubt the verdict."[30]

In early August several more faced trials and were found guilty: George Jacobs, Sr., Martha Carrier, George Burroughs, John and Elizabeth Proctor, and John Willard. John Proctor and George Burroughs were the first men accused of witchcraft (or wizardry) in the area. Proctor was accused first, and is a central character in *The Crucible*. Both were strong-willed men, which may have had something to do with being accused.

John Proctor had been first accused along with his wife in early April. Mary Warren, who had become afflicted early in the crisis, worked for the Proctors. After John Proctor threatened to beat the affliction out of her, Mary was "cured." This was an obvious threat to the accusers, who might also be questioned why they, too, did not recover.[31] Mary Warren was later accused of being a witch. John Proctor had questioned the trials from the beginning.

While in jail, John Proctor wrote a letter to some Boston ministers. He said the judges and accusers had too much control over the situation. He wrote that he and others had been condemned before even going to trial. He also wrote that several people who had confessed did so only after being tortured.[32] Hoffer writes about the letter, "He got nowhere, but it was a measure of the man that he tried."[33] Perhaps it was this testament to his character that drew Arthur Miller to make Proctor a primary character in his play. In *The Crucible*, John Proctor ultimately stays true to what he knows is right rather than falsely admitting to guilt.

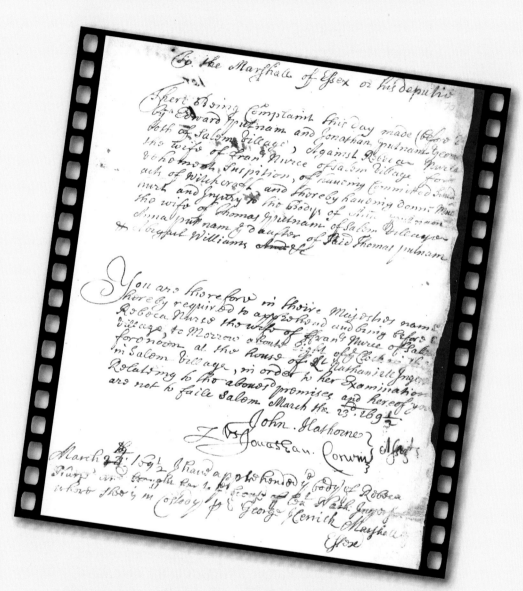

The arrest warrant for Rebecca Nurse. Her staunch, devout manner impressed the jury, which at first declared her not guilty. They later rescinded the verdict and sentenced her to death.

George Burroughs was first accused toward the end of April. He had previously served Salem Village as the minister. Mercy Lewis, one of the primary accusers, had worked for him during that time. In the spring of 1692, she claimed that his specter had visited her and asked her to sign his book, which she had never seen before in his home. She also said he promised her wealth and earthly goods if she signed, which she refused to do.

Burroughs was short but very strong—so much so that some questioned whether his strength was humanly possible. On the other hand, it would not be surprising for a wizard to possess such strength. Burroughs had also survived more than one Indian raid, which also made him suspect. He was in his third marriage, and some suspected that he had beaten his wives, leading to the death of his previous wife. All of these things, combined with his arrogant and outspoken manner, made him a natural target.

When Tituba first told her tales of what she had seen, describing a "black man," some had presumed this to be the devil. Others thought that the man she mentioned was the leader of all the witches. George Burroughs fit the description (since people of the time used the term "black" to mean "swarthy," not "black" in a racial sense).

At his hanging, Burroughs delivered a perfect recitation of the Lord's Prayer, which apparently moved the audience. Cotton Mather, a witness to the execution, stepped in and reminded everyone that Burroughs was a former minister and that no one should be surprised at his ability. Mather also reminded the crowd that Burroughs had been convicted by the court. However, the event captivated the audience, and doubt continued to spread. Additionally, people who had confessed earlier began to recant, or take back, their confessions. Margaret Jacobs, who had accused Burroughs, recanted. She had met with him prior to his execution and asked for forgiveness, which Burroughs gave.[34] He and the others were executed on August 19.

Letters from Jail

Another powerful force causing growing doubt came in the form of another letter written by Mary Easty. She was tried on September 9, along with Martha Corey, Alice Parker, Ann Pudeator, Dorcas Hoar, and Mary Bradbury. Easty lived in Topsfield, and while well respected, her family had been involved with the Putnams in some land disputes over the years.

During her pretrial on April 22, Mary Easty remained calm and answered the questions directed at her. She maintained her innocence throughout. She was so earnest, in fact, that Hathorne asked the accusers at one point if they were certain Easty was the one tormenting them. Not surprisingly, the accusers immediately went into fits of hysteria. Following the trial, however, all the accusers except for Mercy Lewis started backing down from their claims against Easty. As a result, the court released her from jail on May 18. After Easty's release, Mercy Lewis had such terrible fits that she nearly died.[35] At Lewis's bedside, Ann Putnam, Jr., and Abigail Williams said they saw Easty's specter tormenting Lewis.[36] To some researchers this implied that the accusers had collaborated, or decided together,

George Burroughs, the former minister in Salem Village, was hanged despite his ability to say the Lord's Prayer flawlessly.

that they would again accuse Easty. Following this
episode, Easty went back to jail.

Easty wrote two letters while in jail. The first she
wrote with her sister Sarah Cloyce to the judges, saying
that the judges should provide them with counsel and
allow them a fair trial. They wrote:

> Our humble request is first that [seeing] we are
> neither able to plead our [own] cause, nor is
> [counsel] allowed to those in our condition; that
> you who are our Judges, would please to be of
> [counsel] to us, to direct us wherein we may stand
> in [need].[37]

They asked to be able to have others testify in court
for them. They also asked that the court consider more
solid evidence, such as their reputations, rather than
invisible evidence, such as specters. They asked for a
"[fair] and [equal] hearing of what may be [said] for us,
as well as against us."[38]

Easty's second letter, in combination with the first,
may have helped solidify any doubt that people were
feeling. The second letter, addressed to the courts
and to Governor Phips, had both an emotional and a
logical impact. Hoffer writes, "Its force . . . is undeniable,
even after three hundred years."[39] In the letter, Easty
addressed some of the most troubling aspects of the
trials. She did not ask to have her sentence changed.
Instead, she pleaded for the lives of any to follow her,
writing, "I know I must die and my appointed time is
[set] but the Lord he [knows] it is that if it be possible no
more [innocent] blood may be shed . . . "[40] She under-
stood the judges were doing their best to determine the
cause of the afflictions but also asked in her petition

to them that they interrogate the accusers separately to determine if their stories matched. The accusers were always questioned together. They could watch one another for signs and react accordingly.

Easty also spoke of her innocence and her confidence that as she faced the Lord, she would not be condemned. She could not lie and put her soul in jeopardy. Lastly, she said she did not doubt that the Lord "will give a blessing to your [endeavors]."[41]

Easty's letters made an impression and caused people to wonder if innocent people had been and were being executed. It did not halt her execution, though. On September 22, 1692, she was hanged for the crime of witchcraft. The others to hang with her were Martha Corey, Margaret Scott, Alice Parker, Ann Pudeator, Wilmott Redd, Samuel Wardell, and Mary Parker. They were the last people hanged in Salem during the crisis, and the last people executed in North America for the crime of witchcraft.

Nineteen people had been hanged. Sarah Osborne died in jail. Sarah Good's infant baby died in jail, as well as Roger Toothaker, Ann Foster, and Lydia Dustin. And Giles Corey was pressed to death.

Corey refused to stand trial. His reasons could be many. Perhaps one of them was that anyone found guilty of witchcraft lost their personal goods. If he did not stand trial, he could not be condemned, and therefore, he could deed his belongings to his sons. If condemned, he and his family would lose his belongings.[42] Hoffer writes that Giles Corey entered a plea of not guilty but then refused to take part in the trial.[43] The property issue may have been a factor, but others likely played a role as well.

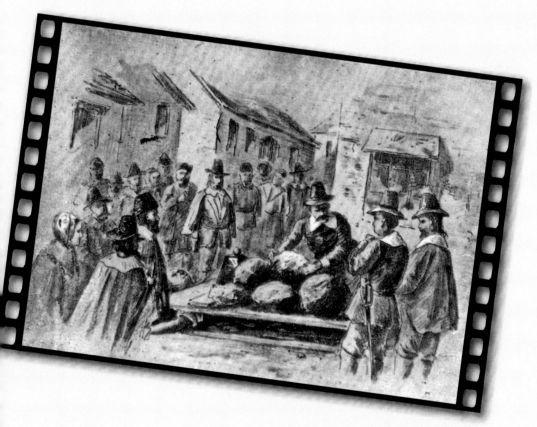

Giles Corey was the only one executed who did not hang.
He was pressed to death under heavy stones in an attempt
to make him talk and participate in his trial.

After several months in miserable jail conditions, and witnessing the same outcome in each trial, Corey may have had enough.

In order to pressure Corey into entering a plea, the court used a particularly gruesome method of persuasion. At almost eighty years old, he was placed under a board in a field near the jail. Large stones were added on top of the board, pressing the man underneath. Over the course of two days, Corey did not enter a plea.[44] His last words are said to have been "More weight." Finally he died, his rib cage crushed under the tremendous weight, days before his wife faced Gallows Hill.

Giles Corey's last stand against the proceedings may have influenced their coming to an end as well. His wife, Martha, faced her execution on September 22 along with the others, but this act of defiance added to the other signs that something had gone terribly wrong in Salem. Hoffer writes, "By dying under the stones, Corey was testifying to his good name. He became part of the legend of the tragedy of Salem, perhaps more than any of his fellow defendants."[45]

Chapter 5

The Aftermath

While the last executions took place on September 22, it was several more months before the witchcraft trials came to an end. A combination of events helped bring the crisis to a close. Some of these events included ongoing doubts of community members, Nathaniel Saltonstall's stepping down from the court, John Proctor's letter, the letters from Mary Easty and Sarah Cloyce, George Burroughs's speech at his execution, and a letter written by a longtime critic of the trials, Thomas Brattle. In addition, rumors circulated that the accusers planned on targeting some well-known people in the community. These included Judge Corwin's mother-in-law and wives of prominent ministers.

However, an outcry from the community's leaders was necessary for change to take place.

Some people, such as Cotton Mather, continued supporting the hearings, even though more people were retracting (taking back) their confessions. Additionally, more and more people had confessed as it became obvious that anyone who confessed would not be executed. To Cotton Mather, the confessions confirmed that the devil was still at work in Salem. The confessions were becoming problematic, though, both in the numbers of people confessing and the numbers of people recanting their confessions. Cotton Mather supported his friend William Stoughton. Other ministers in the surrounding areas were not so sure that witchcraft was as prevalent as it seemed, however. They contacted Cotton's father, Increase Mather.

Increase was a prominent member of society and the president of Harvard College. He was well respected and had helped reinstate the Royal Charter. He was a natural person to step forth and provide an opinion on the proceedings. After receiving input from other ministers, Increase delivered a sermon against the trials on October 3, which was later publicized. His statement marked the turning point in bringing the trials to a close. He spoke out against the ways the trials were handled and decried the use of spectral evidence. In a now famous line he said, "It would be better that ten witches go free than the blood of a single innocent be shed."[1]

Others objected to the trials as well but did not have the influence of Increase Mather. Thomas Brattle had opposed the trials throughout. In a letter to a colleague dated October 8, 1692, he wrote that the trials had been

Cotton Mather was in favor of continuing the trials despite the retracted confessions and the growing doubts in the community.

conducted poorly. He had many complaints about the methods used, such as the touch test. He noted that the accusers were in perfect health aside from their fits. He also wrote that the confessions of the accused could not be taken seriously. Lastly, he condemned the use of spectral evidence.[2] The letter was made public a few days after Increase Mather's sermon. While Brattle's letter probably did not have much to do with the termination of the court, it shows that some people were opposed to the trials and the way they were conducted.

Remembering the Lives Lost

When it all ended, legal action had been taken against at least 144 people, thirty-eight of them men. Fifty-four people confessed to witchcraft, and fourteen women and five men were hanged.[3] Giles Corey was pressed to death.

A Composite Character

In the movie *The Crucible*, Reverend Hale plays a significant role. While not historically accurate, the character embodies a number of different people. Hale leaves the court, for example, representing the real Nathaniel Saltonstall. In the movie he gradually changes his mind about the trials, much like the real Hale, who later wrote regrets about the proceedings.

Those hanged on Gallows Hill were:

June 10: Bridget Bishop.

July 19: Sarah Good, Elizabeth Howe, Susannah Martin, Rebecca Nurse, and Sarah Wildes.

August 19: George Burroughs, Martha Carrier, George Jacobs, John Proctor, and John Willard.

September 22: Martha Corey, Mary Easty, Alice Parker, Mary Parker, Ann Pudeator, Margaret Scott, Wilmott Redd, and Samuel Wardell.

Each name represents a separate and unique story. This book only deals with a few individuals, such as those who were inspiration for characters in *The Crucible* or those whose stories stand out to illustrate a point. Many books and other writings have been devoted to the Salem witch trials, and many go into each person's story in detail.

Legal Significance

The Salem witch trials helped shape the American justice system. As historian Peter Charles Hoffer noted, some of the most basic elements of the American legal system came from the statement by Increase Mather. Important concepts such as "reasonable doubt" and what types of evidence are allowed in a trial help make the process as fair and unbiased as possible. Other ideas that many people may take for granted also stem from the Salem crisis.

At the time of the Salem witch trials, separation of church and state as it is thought of today did not exist. New Englanders supported a legal system separate from the church (which is why they fled England in the first place); however, laws could change depending on the religion of the monarch in England (Catholic or Protestant). In the years leading up to the Salem witch trials, uncertainties in England and New England created legal uncertainties. The official charter was signed during the crisis. The popular phrase "separation of church and state" came into existence later, but the ideas behind it are included in the First Amendment of the United States Constitution, which states, "Congress shall make no law respecting an establishment of religion, or prohibiting the free exercise thereof; or abridging the freedom of speech, or of the press; or the right of the people peaceably to assemble, and to petition the Government for a redress of grievances." In other words, people are free to practice their religious beliefs as long as they do not violate any other laws. Further, people have the right to take a grievance, or legal issue, to the government, or courts. Because people practice different religious beliefs, the government is a separate entity.

The Salem witch trials helped shape the American justice system. Important concepts such as "reasonable doubt" and what types of evidence are allowed in a trial help make the process as fair as possible.

The Court of Oyer and Terminer shut down on October 29, 1692. Turmoil still continued. Neighbors who had accused one another and sent family members to their deaths now had to work and worship side by side. The Reverend Samuel Parris still had some supporters in the church for a couple of years but was

One of those who regretted the conduct of the witchcraft trials was Judge Samuel Sewell, who made a public apology in front of his church's congregation in 1697.

forced out of town in 1696.[4] Author and historian Mary Beth Norton writes, "Within five years, one judge and twelve jurors formally apologized for their roles in the affair, and within two decades the Massachusetts government also acknowledged its responsibility for what were by then viewed as unjust proceedings."[5] At the age of nineteen, Ann Putnam, Jr., issued an apology through the church. In it she blamed the devil for her actions, saying that he had influenced her to act the way she had. Although she did not claim personal responsibility, she did apologize, which the other accusers had not done. Samuel Sewall, one of the officials of the court, later blamed the death of his two-year-old daughter on the trials. In his mind God was punishing him for his role in the trials.[6]

In 1693 Governor Phips pardoned the accused people still in jail. Editor Marc Mappen writes in *Witches and Historians: Interpretations of Salem*, "It was now widely accepted that a tragic error had been made."[7] In 1697 the state of Massachusetts declared January 15 a day of fasting, on which people asked for divine guidance. Samuel Sewall apologized on that day, as did the jurors.[8] Within a few years after the trials, the Massachusetts legislature voted to provide monetary compensation to the survivors of the trials as well as the family members of those who had been jailed or hanged.[9] Governor Phips and Cotton Mather also apologized; however, William Stoughton never did.[10] The accusers faced no formal punishment for their actions. They continued to live in the community, alongside friends and family members of those who had perished.

Chapter 6

The Crucible: Highlights and History

The movie (and play) *The Crucible* is not historically accurate; however, this does not mean that the story does not have merit. Written by the award-winning playwright Arthur Miller, it is considered a great work by many.

Miller was born in Harlem in 1915. The son of Polish immigrants, he watched his parents struggle during and after the Great Depression. Miller eventually studied at the University of Michigan, where he started writing for the theatre. He wrote the play version of *The Crucible* in 1953 in response to what he saw as a modern-day witch hunt: the pursuit and persecution of suspected Communists in the United States.

In 1950 Senator Joseph McCarthy delivered a speech in which he said he knew of over two hundred Communists in the State Department. His accusations led to several years of congressional hearings in which many people were accused of Communist activity. Many people in Hollywood were accused; in turn, those people had trouble finding work. Some also testified against others in order to be spared themselves.

Miller wrote the screenplay for *The Crucible* in 1996, at the age of eighty-one. His life is chronicled in his autobiography, *Timebends: A Life,* published in 1987, in which he discusses his motives behind the play. He died in 2005, after receiving numerous awards for his work, including the Pulitzer Prize.

The Crucible Plot Summary

The movie opens with Abigail Williams, Betty Parris, Mercy Lewis, Mary Warren, and Tituba dancing in the woods. Abigail performs a spell in hopes of killing John Proctor's wife, Elizabeth. Abigail, who had worked as a servant for the Proctors, had an affair with John when Elizabeth was ill. She learned of the affair and let Abigail go. The morning after the dancing, Betty Parris falls ill, as does the Putnam's daughter, Ruth. (Ann Putnam, Jr., is not a character.) Before long, several girls are afflicted, and Martha Corey and Rebecca Nurse are accused of witchcraft.

Thomas Putnam, John Proctor, Giles Corey, and Reverend Samuel Parris argue about Parris's pay,

The Crucible opens with a group of girls dancing in the woods with Tituba. This scene was imagined by Arthur Miller; it is not supported by historical evidence.

property lines, and other issues. Putnam accuses Proctor of stealing wood. Reverend Hale comes to investigate the afflictions, and Tituba confesses to witchcraft, as does Abigail. She names people they saw with the devil but continues to be afflicted. Elizabeth Proctor is arrested, and Martha Corey and Rebecca Nurse are convicted in court. Giles Corey claims that Thomas Putnam is accusing others in order to get their land, and Mary Warren says that she pretended to see specters and falsely accused others. However, Corey does not cooperate with the court, and so he is pressed to death.

Abigail claims that Mary Warren's spirit is hurting her in court. John Proctor calls Abigail a liar, though he admits to the affair with her. Elizabeth Proctor is brought in later and asked if she knows about the affair, which she denies, not knowing that her husband admitted it. Under pressure from Abigail, Mary Warren says she did not lie and blames John Proctor. He is sentenced to die. Before hanging, he confesses, but then decides that he cannot lie and recants his confession. He is sent to Gallows Hill with Rebecca Nurse and Martha Corey.

U.S. Communism and Joseph McCarthy

In the 1940s and 1950s tensions were high in the United States. The Second World War ended in 1945 and the Cold War began. "Cold War" was the term given to tensions and distrust between the United States and the Soviet Union. Both were considered superpowers, and both aimed to have the biggest nuclear weapons program. On occasion, each threatened to use those weapons—or accused the other country of having plans to do so.

Just as the people in Salem were weary from ongoing threats of war from France, the Indians, or both, so, too, were some people in the United States concerned about another major war. This was combined with fears that important political or scientific information might be leaked to the Soviet Union through spies or dishonorable government employees. Out of these fears grew a "witch hunt" for anyone associated with, or sympathetic to, Communist views.

The House Un-American Activities Committee, or HUAC, formed in 1938 to monitor foreign agents. It gained fame in the 1940s and 1950s, when it used forceful tactics to gain information about persons suspected of Communist activities. In 1947, the committee accused a group of movie actors and writers with being associated with Communism. This group became known as the Hollywood Ten.

In 1950 Senator Joseph McCarthy began an investigation into Communist activities in the United States. Claiming to have a list of Communists in the government, he began an intensive interrogation that began in February 1950 and lasted until his censure by the Senate in December 1954. He was pushy and scared many people he questioned. One of his tactics was to make it known to witnesses that in order to clear their own names, they had to name others whom they knew or suspected were involved with Communism. By 1952 McCarthy was investigating "un-American" books and their authors, and later people in the military. The U.S. Army investigations were televised, which showed McCarthy's methods. Eventually, politicians were embarrassed by McCarthy's actions and voted to stop his interrogations in 1954. He died in 1957. "McCarthyism" became a term used to describe personal attacks on people in public without any evidence.

The HUAC continued without the assistance of McCarthy. In 1955 and 1956 Congress called Arthur Miller to identify writers whom he suspected of being Communists or sympathetic to the party. Miller refused, and he was convicted of contempt of Congress. The conviction was overturned in 1958. When he wrote *The Crucible* in 1953, he could not have known that these events were coming. The play parallels some of his observations of the HUAC activities, however. It also sheds light on Miller's views of what can happen when people become impassioned about something, and how easy it can be to turn to blame rather than work together as a community.

The play was first performed at the height of the McCarthy era, and it was not well received, perhaps in part out of fear. It was more accepted in the 1960s, and it has become one of his best-known plays since that time. Millions of copies of the play were sold, and countless productions were mounted. In his autobiography, *Timebends*, Miller wrote about the culture in the United States during the time of the Communist investigations, referring to them at one point as "the Communist witch-hunt."[1] He also described the atmosphere surrounding the hearings. "Swirling about the hearings was a moral confusion that no one seemed able to penetrate and clarify, even by bending history now and then."[2] Prior to writing *The Crucible*, Miller described the HUAC activities and his feelings about them. His descriptions of

Playwright Arthur Miller talks with actor Daniel Day-Lewis on the set of *The Crucible*. The play shows Miller's ideas about what can happen when a community is overcome by fear and emotion.

those events could have been used to portray the Salem Trials. He focused particularly on issues of the government, saying that people involved in investigating Communists were morally guilty and should know better. Miller also wrote about the idea that a person could lessen feelings of guilt by naming others. In comparing the HUAC investigations and the Salem witch trials, Miller wrote, "The rituals of guilt and confession followed all the forms of a religious inquisition, except, of course, that the offended parties were not God and his ministers but a congressional committee."[3]

The Crucible was first performed at the height of the McCarthy era, and it was not well received, perhaps in part out of fear.

Miller did extensive research on the Salem trials when writing *The Crucible*, which he said took a year to write. While the HUAC hearings inspired the play and the connections are obvious, Miller sought to capture the feelings of the trials on an individual level. He wrote that when thinking about the play, one theme kept coming back. Of his main character's fictionalized activities and emotions, Miller wrote that John Proctor was "a guilt-ridden man . . . who, having slept with his teenage servant girl, watches with horror as she becomes the leader of the witch-hunting pack and points her accusing finger at the wife he has himself betrayed."[4]

The play, a fictionalized account of the real Salem trials, certainly has parallels to the HUAC hearings.

It also examines human behavior. Why do people act the way they do? How do people react to their own feelings of guilt? Why do people accuse others of wrongdoing? These are questions that may never have definite answers but are the kinds of questions raised by the Salem witch trials. Why did the accusers do what they did? Many historians have tried to answer that question, but no definitive answers have emerged.

Concerning historical accuracy, Miller knew that he was not presenting the play as the events actually happened. This was a fictional play based on the events in Salem. It mirrored current events and provided an opportunity to explore human behavior. When faced with the argument that comparing the two events would not work because there actually were Communists in modern America but no witches in Salem, Miller wrote that he believed that Tituba had actually practiced some type of magic with the girls.[5] He also wrote that the two events had similar themes:

> The political question, therefore, of whether witches and Communists could be equated was no longer to the point. What was . . . parallel was the guilt, two centuries apart, of holding . . . feelings of alienation and hostility toward standard, daylight society. . . . [6]

Responses to *The Crucible*

When Miller wrote *The Crucible*, he had already established himself as a noteworthy playwright. *Death of a Salesman*, one of his best-known and acclaimed works, received positive reviews when it came out in 1949. In a time when actors and writers might lose their

Mary Warren (played by Karron Graves) is confronted by Judge Thomas Danforth (played by Paul Scofield), in this scene from *The Crucible*.

jobs after refusing to name others or simply by being suspected of Communism, *The Crucible* was "a bold as well as timely play, written at a time when the congressional investigators had the power to do considerable damage."[7] This viewpoint by writer Henry Popkin introduced his ideas about the play. While the play has historical inaccuracies, Popkin argues that Miller had to include more than the historical facts in order to create drama. This is because in the literary sense a tragedy is usually brought about by the main character or characters. In the Salem trials, the accused were innocent targets.[8]

To add a tragic literary element to *The Crucible*, Miller used John Proctor's guilt over betraying his wife. This allowed the tragedy to unfold as a result of the character's actions. He had an affair, and that led Abigail Williams to accuse Elizabeth Proctor of witchcraft. Proctor wants his servant, Mary Warren, to admit that she and the other girls were faking their symptoms and never saw any spirits. This leads Proctor to call Abigail a liar. To determine whether John Proctor or Abigail Williams is lying, the judge asks Proctor's wife whether she knows of the affair. John Proctor states that his wife would not lie. However, to defend her husband's honor, she lies, which lands John Proctor in jail under accusations of cavorting with the devil. The Puritans had strict beliefs about lying. God would punish a liar. Elizabeth lies, and later John lies and admits to being in league with the devil. However, he ultimately decides that he only has his name left and will not publicly admit to witchcraft. He then faces the gallows.

Daniel Day-Lewis as John Proctor rides to the gallows with the other convicted witches.

The play deals with more issues than guilt and tragedy, however. Not surprisingly, given the background of the times in which Miller wrote the play, it also deals with issues of power. Author Christopher Bigsby writes that Miller does not try to explain why the girls in the play or in Salem acted the way they did. Miller does, however, clearly make a point about the influence of power that the young girls have over others. Bigsby writes, "Power, certainly, is an issue in *The Crucible* but it is not in the hands of the rich landowners. It is in the hands of young girls who contest the order of the world."[9] Under normal circumstances, it would not have been possible for a group of young girls to have power over adults and the courts, as they did not have a power-holding place in society. In the play, they manipulate the fears of the community to exert this power. In the real Salem trials, adults as well as children served as accusers. Adult men submitted the official complaints against the accused. However, Miller used the idea that a group of otherwise powerless people could exert power and influence over others.

Many regard *The Crucible* as one of Miller's greatest works. It has remained in production since it was written, and the movie received many positive reviews. This says something not only about the quality of the work but also the message it delivers about human nature. Repeatedly, people have banded together to blame others, creating hysteria and fear. This occurred not only in Salem but also in 1950s America. It has happened across the globe, throughout all time. Can these types of witch hunts continue today? And if so, can the law protect people now better than it did in 1692?

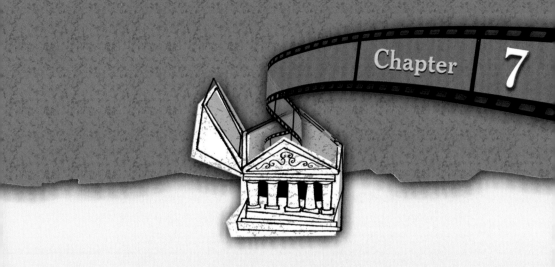

Chapter 7

Does History Repeat Itself?

It is still unknown why the accusers in Salem acted the way they did. Historians have proposed various theories. Some believe that the girls acted maliciously; that is, they believe the accusers were faking their symptoms in order to take revenge on people they disliked or who they felt had done them wrong. The idea that the girls faked their symptoms was a long-held belief, in part because the Reverend John Hale hinted at this in his recollections of the trials.

Others believe the accusers were having fun of sorts. They were able to gain attention and have some control and power over their lives and the lives of others. However, if their symptoms were exaggerated, or done knowingly, it is possible the girls did not realize the seriousness of their actions until it was too late. At that point they were unable to recant, as this would have placed them in jeopardy. If they admitted they were lying, they could have faced the gallows.

Some have argued, such as author Carol F. Karlsen, that the issue went much deeper than simply "sport," as one of the accusers called it. Karlsen notes that most of the accused were women and examines why this was the case. While there were more men accused in Salem than was typical in the European witch crisis, only five of the nineteen people hanged in Salem were men. Were the accusations the result of hatred against a certain type of woman? Even though the afflicted persons were mostly young girls, the trials would not have happened as they did if men had not taken part. Those involved in the legal proceedings were men, as were those who had a direct influence on the community's reactions and beliefs—ministers such as Samuel Parris and Cotton Mather spoke out continuously that the devil worked in Salem, and that he could disguise himself any way he chose. Karlsen named her book *The Devil in the Shape of a Woman*. Puritan beliefs placed women below men, and some types of women, many whom were accused, fit a certain profile, such as being older, single (unmarried or widowed), poor or rich (either could work against her), and outspoken. Not all the women accused fit this profile, of course, but there are some patterns in the accusations.

John Proctor (center) and two women are hanged in the movie *The Crucible*. For three centuries, people have wondered why such horrific events took place in Salem.

Some people believe that the girls truly were afflicted, perhaps not by witchcraft directly, but by the belief in witchcraft. The mind can be a powerful thing, and if the girls believed they were being attacked, they may have seen and felt the things they claimed. Certain types of mental illnesses cause hallucinations and hysteria, which the girls could have interpreted as specters trying to harm them. Other experts have suggested physical illnesses, but those theories have not held up.

What happened after the trials? The Salem witch trials occurred early in United States history—only a few years after the establishment of that settlement and eighty-four years before the Declaration of Independence. However, it can be argued that the trials helped shape, to some degree, the future of the United States legal system. As Peter Charles Hoffer noted, the sermon by Increase Mather in opposition to the trials had some elements of future legal terms and ideas. These ideas helped determine what types of evidence are allowed in the court, the role of witnesses, and the concept of condemning someone only if the evidence shows guilt "beyond a reasonable doubt."

The trials also helped shape later ideas of separation of church and state. Under 1692 English law, the church and the state were one. Heresy was punishable by death. The authors of the U.S. Constitution took care to separate religion from the legal system and to introduce a system of checks and balances. The government has three branches, each designed to keep the other in check. The legal system includes such protections as allowable evidence, witnesses, and juries of peers.

The legal system is in place to protect people in a fair manner.

Additionally, the system is designed to protect and serve both accusers (prosecutors) and those accused (defendants). While the legal system has evolved over time, adapting to the needs of the people, the original system was designed to provide a fair and consistent process. The lessons learned from the Salem witch trials helped show why these concepts are necessary.

Did they make a difference? Could someone be accused of witchcraft today? No matter how well designed a legal system is, there is still the possibility of error. It may seem unlikely that in modern society someone could be accused and prosecuted for cavorting with the devil. However, this is exactly what happened in California in 1983. In this case, the owners of the McMartin Preschool in Manhattan Beach, California, were accused of child abuse. This was based on reports of some of the children, who described horrific accounts of abuse that were interpreted as satanic rituals. Supposedly, at least forty children were harmed. The owners of the preschool were arrested and charged. Several years later, after millions of dollars spent trying the case and two hung juries, the case was dropped.[1] This case shows how the words of a child combined with the understandable fears of a parent or social worker can quickly grow out

> Some people believe that the girls truly were afflicted, perhaps not by witchcraft directly, but by the belief in witchcraft.

of control. In the process many innocent people were affected. To some this case was similar to the events in Salem. It was brought about by the words of children, it quickly grew out of control, and few spoke out against the claims.

In the late 1990s, Peter Charles Hoffer wrote:

> It has happened over and over after Salem. In Barbados and in Nigeria, Tituba's homes before Salem, witches are still feared and persecuted. In the 1990s, suspected witches by the hundreds—the actual number may never be known—were summarily executed by angry neighbors in South Africa. The suspects were older women and men, and the pattern of suspicion and accusation differed little from that in Salem.[2]

What about today in the United States? In the 1950s and in the California case in the 1980s, the term witch hunt was used to describe events in which one group singles out another based on fears and suspicions. In recent years, news articles have used the term when referring to antiterrorist activities. In writing about the government's investigations of possible suspects in the United States, columnist Robert Scheer wrote: "What we don't need is a witch hunt against the American people, ferreting through their private lives or detaining them because of their ethnicity."[3]

Is it possible to learn from history? When a group of people seems threatening, taking care of the issue in some way often feels justified. However, the Salem witch trials showed that jumping to conclusions and relying on poor evidence can have serious outcomes. Hopefully, the deaths of those who were hanged on Gallows Hill will serve as a reminder.

CHAPTER NOTES

 Satan in Salem

1. Paul Boyer and Stephen Nissenbaum, eds., *The Salem Witchcraft Papers: Verbatim Transcripts of the Legal Documents of the Salem Witchcraft Outbreak of 1692* (New York: Da Capo Press, 1977), vol. II, pp. 657–662.
2. Marilynne K. Roach, *The Salem Witch Trials: A Day-by-Day Chronicle of a Community Under Siege* (Lanham, Md.: Taylor Trade Publishing, 2002), pp. 69–73.
3. Peter Charles Hoffer, *The Salem Witchcraft Trials: A Legal History* (Lawrence, Kans.: University Press of Kansas, 1997), p. I.

 The Crime of Witchcraft

1. P. G. Maxwell-Stuart, *Witchcraft: A History* (Stroud, UK: Tempus Publishing, 2000–04), p. 21.
2. Albert Van Helden, "The Inquisition," *The Galileo Project, 1995,* <http://galileo.rice.edu/chr/inquisition.html> (April 9, 2007).
3. Jeffrey B. Russell, *A History of Witchcraft. Sorcerers, Heretics and Pagans* (New York: Thames and Hudson, 1980, reprinted 1987), p. 70.
4. Van Helden.
5. "In Search of History: Salem Witch Trials," The History Channel, DVD, 1998, A&E Television Networks.
6. Russell, p. 70.
7. Ibid., pp. 72, 83.
8. Ibid., p. 68.
9. Maxwell-Stuart, p. 73.

10. Russell, p. 69.
11. Marilynne K. Roach. *The Salem Witch Trials: A Day-by-Day Chronicle of a Community Under Siege* (Lanham, Md.: Taylor Trade Publishing, 2002), p. xix.
12. Mary Beth Norton, *In the Devil's Snare: The Salem Witchcraft Crisis of 1692* (New York: Vintage Books, 2002), p. 17.
13. Roach, p. xxvii.
14. Ibid., p. xxxlv.
15. Ibid., p. xxxvii.
16. Ibid., p. xliv.

 3 The Path to Court: Legal Issues and Events

1. Mary Beth Norton, *In the Devil's Snare: The Salem Witchcraft Crisis of 1692* (New York: Vintage Books, 2002), p. 19.
2. Peter Charles Hoffer, *The Salem Witchcraft Trials: A Legal History* (Lawrence, Kans.: University Press of Kansas, 1997), p. 36.
3. Norton, pp. 18–19.
4. Marilynne K. Roach, *The Salem Witch Trials: A Day-by-Day Chronicle of a Community Under Siege* (Lanham, Md.: Taylor Trade Publishing, 2002), p. 18.
5. Norton, p. 21.
6. Ibid., p. 22.
7. Roach, p. 21.
8. Norton, p. 25.
9. Ibid., p. 26.
10. Paul Boyer and Stephen Nissenbaum, eds., *The Salem Witchcraft Papers: Verbatim Transcripts of the Legal Documents of the Salem Witchcraft Outbreak of 1692* (New York: Da Capo Press, 1977), vol. II, p. 356.
11. Ibid.
12. Ibid., p. 610.
13. Ibid., pp. 610–611.
14. Norton, p. 27.
15. Boyer, p. 747.
16. Ibid., p. 747.

17. Ibid., p. 757.
18. Norton, p. 29.
19. Ibid., p. 41.

 4 On What Grounds? Evidence and Testimony in Court

1. Marilynne K. Roach, *The Salem Witch Trials: A Day-by-Day Chronicle of a Community Under Siege* (Lanham, Md.: Taylor Trade Publishing, 2002), p. 38.
2. Ibid., p. 40.
3. "Salem Witch Trials: Chronology," *Salem, Massachusetts: The City Guide*, April 21, 2007, <http://www.salemweb.com/memorial/> (April 21, 2007).
4. Chadwick Hansen, *Witchcraft at Salem* (New York: George Braziller, 1969), p. 44.
5. Paul Boyer and Stephen Nissenbaum, eds., *The Salem Witchcraft Papers: Verbatim Transcripts of the Legal Documents of the Salem Witchcraft Outbreak of 1692* (New York: Da Capo Press, 1977), vol. I, p. 249.
6. Hansen, p. 44.
7. Roach, p. 47.
8. Boyer, p. 585.
9. Ibid., p. 586.
10. Hansen, p. 53.
11. Ibid., p. 54.
12. Ibid., p. 53.
13. Roach, p. 66.
14. "Salem Witch Trials: Chronology."
15. Hansen, p. 55.
16. Frances Hill, *A Delusion of Satan: The Full Story of the Salem Witch Trials* (New York: Da Capo Press, 1995), p. 6.
17. Ibid., pp. 22–23.
18. Roach, p. 67.
19. Mary Beth Norton, *In the Devil's Snare: The Salem Witchcraft Crisis of 1692* (New York: Vintage Books, 2002), p. 81.

20. Peter Charles Hoffer, *The Salem Witchcraft Trials: A Legal History* (Lawrence, Kans.: University Press of Kansas, 1997), p. 71.
21. "Salem Witch Trials: Chronology."
22. Hoffer, p. 73.
23. Ibid., p. 74.
24. Ibid., p. 75.
25. Ibid., pp. 82–84.
26. Ibid., p. 85.
27. Ibid., pp. 85–88.
28. Ibid., p. 88.
29. Ibid., p. 105.
30. Ibid., p. 106.
31. Ibid., p. 112.
32. Ibid.
33. Ibid.
34. Ibid., p. 118.
35. Anne Taite Austin, "Biography: Mary Easty," *Salem Witch Trials Documentary Archive Project*, 2001, <http://jefferson.village.virginia.edu:8090/saxon/servlet/SaxonServlet?source=salem/texts/bios.xml&style=salem/xsl/dynaxml.xsl&chunk.id=b8&clear-stylesheet-cache=yes> (April 24, 2007).
36. Ibid.
37. Boyer, p. 302.
38. Ibid., p. 303.
39. Hoffer, p. 102.
40. Boyer, p. 304.
41. Ibid., p. 304.
42. Austin.
43. Hoffer, p. 126.
44. Ibid., p. 127.
45. Ibid.

 5 The Aftermath

1. Matthew Madden, "Biography: Increase Mather," *Salem Witch Trials Documentary Archive Project*, 2001, <http://jefferson.village.virginia.edu:8090/saxon/servlet/Saxon

Servlet?source=salem/texts/bios.xml&style=salem/xsl/
dynaxml.xsl&chunk.id=b15&clear-stylesheet-cache=yes>
(April 26, 2007).

2. "Biography: Thomas Brattle," *Salem Witch Trials Documentary Archive Project,* 2001, <http://jefferson.village. virginia.edu:8090/saxon/servlet/SaxonServlet?source=salem /texts/bios.xml&style=salem/xsl/dynaxml.xsl&chunk.id=b15 &clear-stylesheet-cache=yes> (April 26, 2007).

3. Mary Beth Norton, *In the Devil's Snare: The Salem Witchcraft Crisis of 1692* (New York: Vintage Books, 2002), p. 4.

4. Anne Taite Austin, "Biography: Mary Easty," *Salem Witch Trials Documentary Archive Project,* 2001, <http://jefferson. village.virginia.edu:8090/saxon/servlet/SaxonServlet?source =salem/texts/bios.xml&style=salem/xsl/dynaxml.xsl&chunk .id=b15&clear-stylesheet-cache=yes> (April 26, 2007).

5. Norton, p. 10.

6. Marilynne K. Roach, *The Salem Witch Trials: A Day-by-Day Chronicle of a Community Under Siege* (Lanham, Md.: Taylor Trade Publishing, 2002), p. 550.

7. Marc Mappen, ed., *Witches & Historians: Interpretations of Salem* (Malabar, Fla.: Krieger Publishing Company, 1996), p. 5.

8. Ibid., p. 5.

9. Norton, pp. 10–11.

10. Peter Charles Hoffer, *The Salem Witchcraft Trials: A Legal History* (Lawrence, Kans.: University Press of Kansas, 1997), pp. 140–144.

6 *The Crucible:* Highlights and History

1. Arthur Miller, *Timebends: A Life* (New York: Grove Press, 1987), p. 313.

2. Ibid., p. 329.

3. Ibid., p. 331.

4. Ibid., p. 332.

5. Ibid., pp. 339–340.

6. Ibid., p. 341.

7. Henry Popkin, "Arthur Miller's *The Crucible,*" *College English*, vol. 26, no. 2, November 1964, p. 140.

8. Ibid., pp. 139–146.

9. Christopher Bigsby, *Arthur Miller: A Critical Study* (New York: Cambridge University Press, 2005), p. 154.

 Does History Repeat Itself?

1. "McMartin Preschool Abuse Trials, 1987–1990," *Famous Trials*, n.d., <http://www.law.umkc.edu/faculty/projects/ftrials/mcmartin/mcmartin.html> (April 27, 2007).

2. Peter Charles Hoffer, *The Salem Witchcraft Trials: A Legal History* (Lawrence, Kans.: University Press of Kansas, 1997), p. 145.

3. Robert Scheer, "We've Had Enough Witchhunts," *Los Angeles Times*, June 4, 2002, <http://www.robertscheer.com/1_natcolumn/02_columns/060402.htm> nd, (April 28, 2007).

GLOSSARY

acquittal—Judgment of not guilty; being set free of a legal charge by a verdict or sentence.

capital case—One in which the defendant might be executed if found guilty.

familiar—An animal inhabited by a spirit, doing the work of witches and feeding on their blood.

heresy—An opinion, belief, or action that goes against the doctrine of a particular religion.

heretic—A person who holds beliefs different from his or her religion.

incantation—The use of spells or charms spoken or sung as part of a magic ritual.

Inquisition—A former Roman Catholic practice of discovering and punishing acts of heresy.

magistrate—An official in charge of administering the law.

misogyny—The hatred of women and girls.

Puritans—A Protestant religious group of the sixteenth and seventeenth century in England and New England.

recant—To take back an earlier statement.

sacrament—A religious rite or observance. In Christianity, the taking of Communion is a sacrament.

specter—A spirit or ghostly image of a person.

FURTHER READING

Books

Aronson, Marc. *Witch-Hunt: Mysteries of the Salem Witch Trials.* New York: Atheneum Books for Young Readers, 2003.

Crewe, Sabrina, and Michael V. Uschan. *The Salem Witch Trials.* Milwaukee, Wisc.: Gareth Stevens Publishing, 2005.

Yolen, Jane, and Heidi Stemple. *The Salem Witch Trials: An Unsolved Mystery from History.* New York: Simon and Schuster, 2004.

Internet Addresses

Salem Witch Trials: Documentary Archive and Transcript Project
    <http://etext.virginia.edu/salem/witchcraft/>

"Salem Witch Trials: The World behind the Hysteria"
    <http://school.discoveryeducation.com/schooladventures/salemwitchtrials/>

University of Missouri–Kansas City School of Law Famous Trials in American History "Salem Witchcraft Trials (1692)"
    <http://www.law.umkc.edu/faculty/projects/FTrials/scopes/scopes.htm>

INDEX